# The Movie Kama Sutra

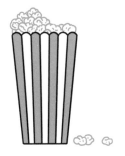

# The Movie Kama Sutra

## 69 SEX POSITIONS FOR MOVIE LOVERS

*Words by*
**ADAM WOODWARD**

*Illustrated by*
**LAURÈNE BOGLIO**

LAURENCE KING PUBLISHING

# Contents

**35. Prom Scream**
Carrie (1976)

**36. Play it Again**
Casablanca (1942)

**37. Hard Shoulder**
Crash (1997)

**38. The Potter's Wheel**
Ghost (1990)

**39. Fright Night**
Nosferatu (1922)

**40. Goosing**
Top Gun (1986)

**41. A Taste of Cherry**
Varsity Blues (1999)

**42. Chest Burster**
Alien (1979)

**43. Project Mayhem**
Fight Club (1999)

**44. Lift Off**
An Officer and a Gentleman (1982)

**45. Rockabye**
Cry-Baby (1990)

**46. Exquisite Corpse**
The Neon Demon (2016)

**47. Rain Check**
The Notebook (2004)

**48. Capote Couture**
Breakfast at Tiffany's (1961)

**49. Automatic Pilot**
Airplane! (1980)

**50. Triple Word Score**
Rosemary's Baby (1968)

**51. What a Feeling**
Flashdance (1983)

**52. Common Courtesy**
Full Metal Jacket (1987)

**53. Doctor, Doctor**
The Silence of the Lambs (1991)

**54. Wicked Game**
Wild at Heart (1990)

**55. Hold the Phone**
Women on the Verge of a
Nervous Breakdown (1988)

**56. In Too Deep**
American Psycho (2000)

**57. Kick it**
Charlie's Angels (2000)

**58. Shower Time**
Psycho (1960)

**59. Delicious Breeze**
The Seven Year Itch (1955)

**60. Executive Assistant**
Secretary (2002)

**61. Man in the Moon**
La Voyage Dans La Lune (1902)

**62. Tunnel of Love**
Carol (2015)

**63. Kiss of Death**
The Godfather: Part II (1974)

**64. Smooth Operator**
True Romance (1993)

**65. Bullet Time**
The Matrix (1999)

**66. Assassins' Tango**
Mr. & Mrs. Smith (2005)

**67. Surf's Up**
Point Break (1991)

**68. The Ballerina**
Black Swan (2010)

**69. The Web Slinger**
Spider-Man (2002)

# King of the World

**Titanic (1997)**

Role-play at its most romantic, this position will give you and your partner the feeling of taking flight. If you don't have a blue-diamond necklace handy, a pearl one will do.

# Reverse Cowboy

**Brokeback Mountain (2005)**

This position is best experienced under a starry night sky. Have your partner lie down on their back and then tenderly straddle them. Spurred boots should be avoided.

# Deli Special

### When Harry Met Sally... (1989)

It's 71 degrees out. Your partner is taking ages to order a sandwich. Now's your chance to spontaneously tease them under the table. Soon they won't be faking anything.

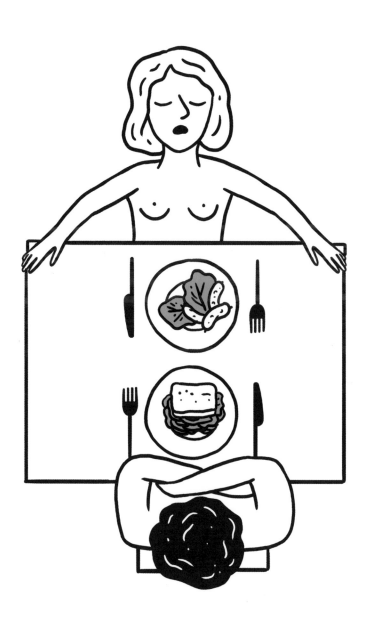

# Heeere's Johnny

### The Shining (1980)

It's important to find the right balance between work and play, otherwise life can become pretty dull. Spread your partner's legs to give them a welcome surprise.

# Time of their Life

### Dirty Dancing (1987)

Have your partner jump into your arms and try to execute a clean catch-and-lift. Practice makes perfect, especially when it comes to the all-important cunnilingus bit.

# Shark Bait

**Jaws (1975)**

Strap on a rubber fin and fellate your partner beneath the waves. If you happen to pick a public beach, you'll want to avoid catching the attention of the local coastguard.

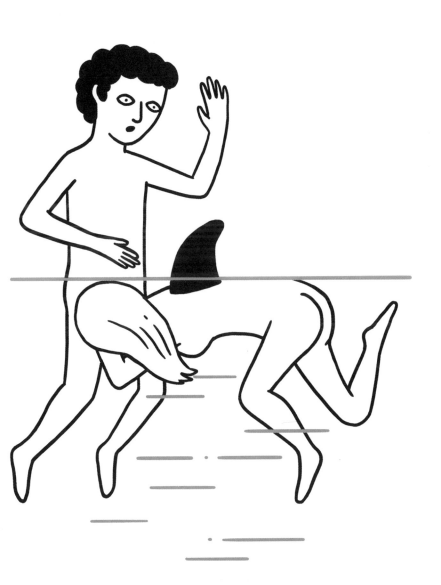

# Sprint Finish

**Forrest Gump (1994)**

You never know what you're gonna get with a new sexual partner; the slightest amount of physical contact could see them pass the finish line a lot sooner than expected.

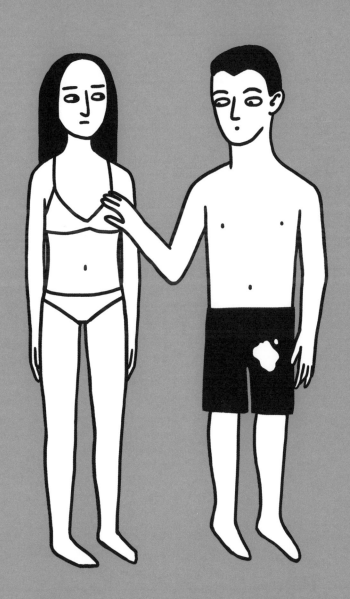

# Venting

**Die Hard (1988)**

Discreetly slip into an air vent that's just big enough for you and your partner to squeeze into. Pretty soon it'll be hotter than Christmas in Los Angeles.

# No Lookin' Back

**Thelma & Louise (1991)**

Whether you're in a hurry or just hanging out, take a moment to capture the special bond between you by taking a selfie together the old-fashioned way.

# Head in a Spin

**The Exorcist (1973)**

'The power of Christ compels you...' to try and face your partner as they take you from behind. Not as easy as it looks, but wickedly fun when you get it right.

# Going Down

**Drive (2011)**

Prove to your partner that you can be a real hero by taking them passionately in a lift before making a clean getaway. And try not to worry about the mess too much.

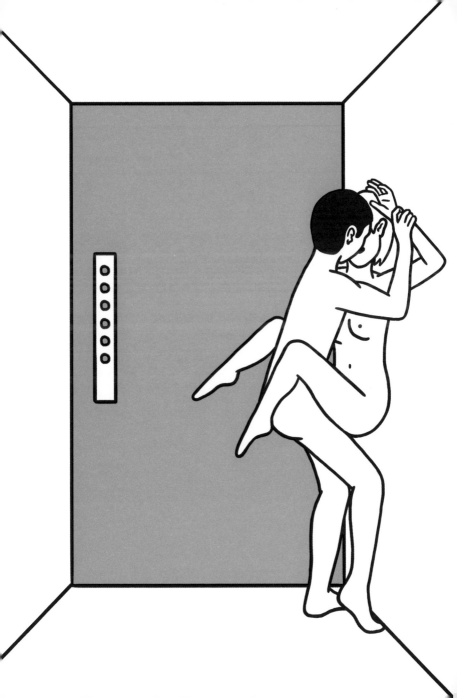

# An Offer they Can't Refuse

**The Godfather (1972)**

Saddle up and let your partner take you for a ride that's guaranteed to leave you both feeling giddy.
A horse's-head mask is essential, stirrups are optional.

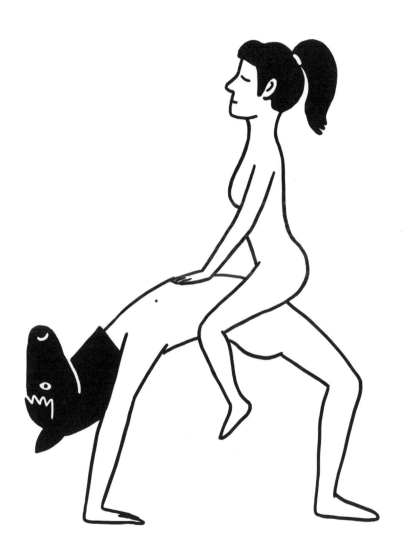

# The Berry Twist

**Pulp Fiction (1994)**

You never can tell how someone's moves on the dancefloor will translate to the bedroom. Find out by giving this fleet-footed position a whirl.

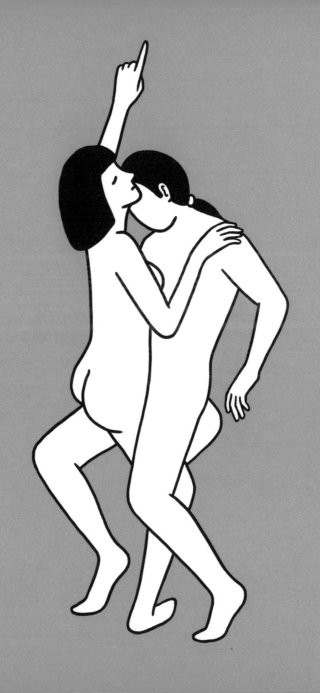

# Casualties of War

**Platoon (1986)**

Wrap your legs around your partner and ride them until their neck is craned backwards and they're reaching for the heavens. Warning: may trigger PTSD flashbacks.

# Speaking Shellfish

**Annie Hall (1977)**

Foodies will love this playful act of culinary copulation.
Use live crustaceans for a genuine thrill, but be prepared
to call the `lobster squad' should things get out of hand.

# Strange Love

**Eyes Wide Shut (1999)**

Host a masquerade ball for you and your more sexually permissive friends. Your local fancy dress shop should stock Venetian masks. Pre-orgy satanic ritual optional.

# Strike Out

**The Big Lebowski (1998)**

Shine up your bowling shoes and slip into a far-out groove, then give your partner some handy pointers on improving their bowling action.

# Flat-pack Fumble

**(500) Days of Summer (2009)**

On your next trip to your local discount furniture retailer, try pretending you're in your own home. Find a quiet corner of the showroom to avoid startling other shoppers.

# Blowing Bubbles

**Waterworld (1995)**

Make sure you're both fully submerged, then embrace your partner for a moment of underwater ecstasy. Just don't leave it too long before coming up for air.

# Stayin' Alive

### Saturday Night Fever (1977)

Most nightclubs frown on overzealous public displays of affection, so stay at home and make your own disco floor. Strike a pose and feel the `movement all around.´

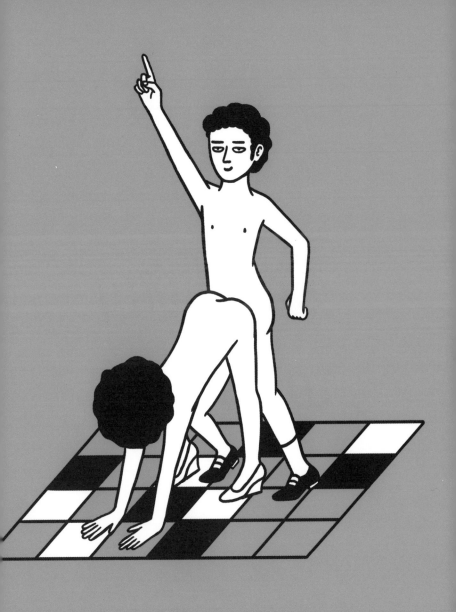

# 21

# Stairway to Heaven

### A History of Violence (2005)

Have you always suspected your partner of having a dark side? See if you can coax it out of them by encouraging them to take you suddenly on the stairs.

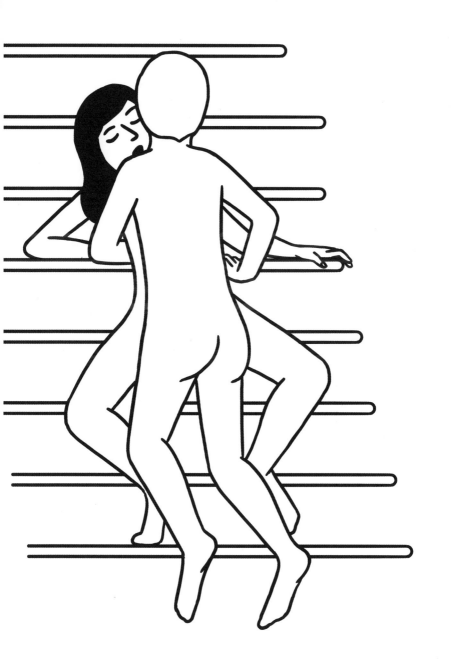

# The Shy Topiarist

### Edward Scissorhands (1990)

Take a pair of scissors and shape your partner's pubic hair into an ornamental artwork. Start with something simple before moving on to more complex designs.

# Hand Solo

**Star Wars: Episode IV – A New Hope (1977)**

Find a quiet spot in a dimly lit cantina, pull up a stool and set to work. Once you start feeling the force of this self-stimulating act, there'll be no questioning who shot first.

# № 24

# Boombox Serenade

**Say Anything… (1989)**

Make a mix tape of 1980s pop ballads, then blast it from a portable stereo as your partner goes down on you. One for hopeless romantics everywhere.

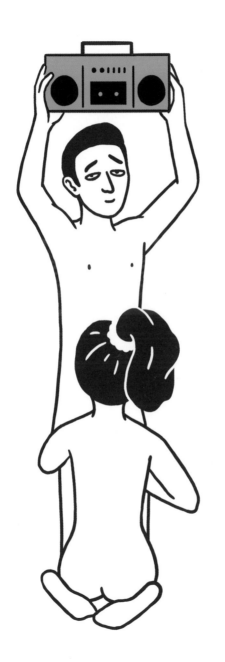

# Yuppie's Delight

**Shame (2011)**

Book a hotel room with a floor-to-ceiling window for you to press your partner up against. Whether you take things fast or slow, remember that no-one likes a greedy lover.

# Bathing Beauty

**Pretty Woman (1990)**

Run a hot bath and give your partner a full head-to-toe sponge-down as you idly shoot the breeze. Then lay back and treat them to a slippery foot job.

MAX
8

# Little Bill's Embarrassment

**Boogie Nights (1997)**

Invite a group of total strangers to stand around you and a partner as you have sex. You'll soon be transported back to LA's San Fernando Valley circa the 1970s.

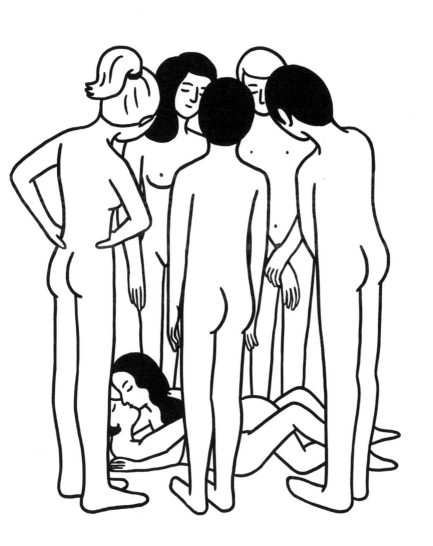

# Whip-Round

**Raiders of the Lost Ark (1981)**

Facing your partner, wrap a braided leather whip tightly around you both. Keep a firm grip and you'll soon both be dripping like a Nazi next to a biblical artifact.

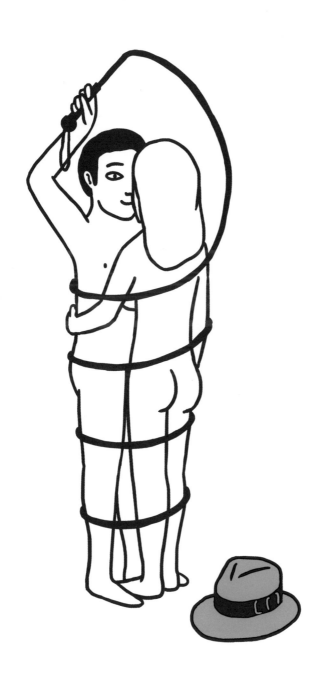

# Salty 'n' Sweet

**Diner (1982)**

Cut a hole in the base of a popcorn bucket and insert yourself into it to give your partner a warm salty treat they won't be expecting. Not recommended for a first date.

# Not My Tempo

**Whiplash (2014)**

Using your partner's backside as a drum, lay down a simple beat before gradually increasing your speed. Just don't get too carried away and start hurling insults at them.

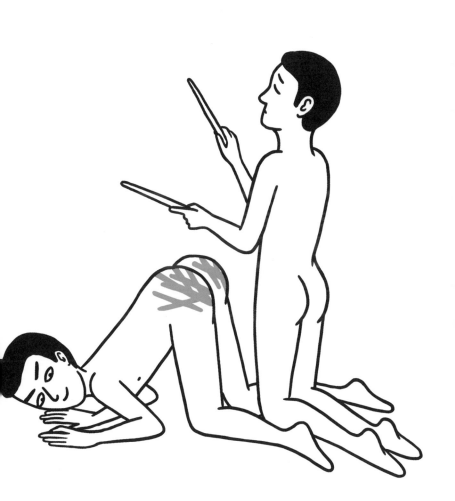

# 31

# Cable Drop

**Mission: Impossible (1996)**

Your mission, should you choose to accept it, is to find
a length of rope strong enough to support your weight.
A stunt position guaranteed to make you sweat.

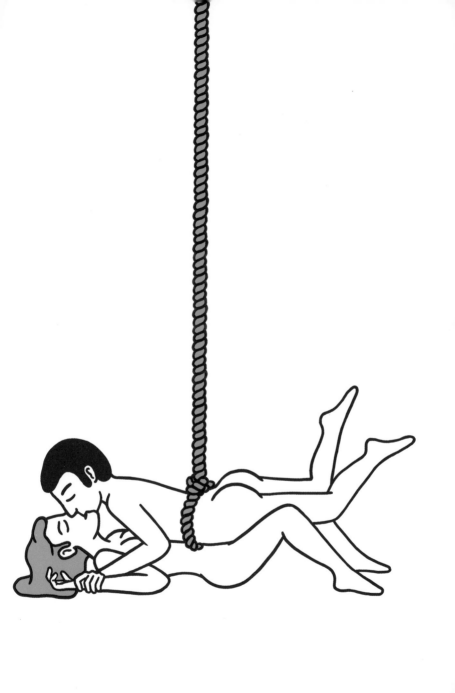

# Kissing Practice

**Cruel Intentions (1999)**

The art of seduction is all about knowing your target.
Once acquired, lock lips and use your tongue to caress
theirs for the steamiest French kiss you'll ever experience.

# What Happens in Vegas

**Showgirls (1995)**

An outdoor swimming pool or jacuzzi is the ideal setting for this wet and wild position. Remember to pack a spare towel, and don't skimp on the bubbles.

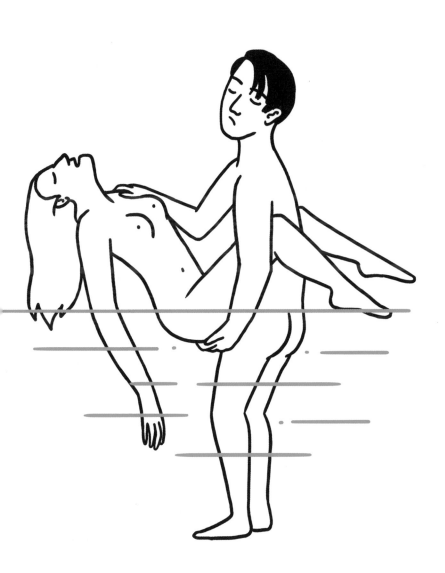

# Desert Island Kicks

**Cast Away (2000)**

A plus side of being stranded on a remote tropical island is that there's no-one around to judge you. Something to remember next time you're feeling lost and lonely.

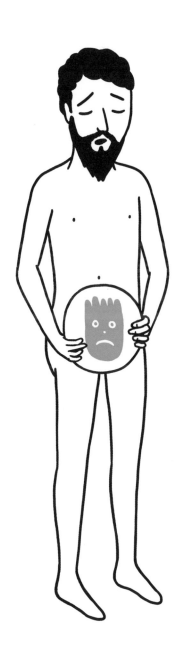

# Prom Scream

**Carrie (1976)**

You don't need to possess telekinetic powers or a fetish
for public humiliation, just the ability to persuade
your partner to ejaculate directly over you from above.

# Play it Again

**Casablanca (1942)**

The world will always welcome lovers who understand what it means to be selfless. This piano-based position also allows you to practise your fingering technique.

# Hard Shoulder

**Crash (1997)**

Indulge your paraphilic tendencies by rubbing yourself against your partner while lying by the side of a road. Avoid penetrating any unnaturally occurring orifices.

# The Potter's Wheel

### Ghost (1990)

Embrace your partner from behind, using your hand to gently caress them. To make things even more interesting, see how long you can keep the clay spinning.

# Fright Night

**Nosferatu (1922)**

Creep up on your partner with your stake poised to plunge. Keep the lights on and maintain complete silence while you act out this horror-inspired sexual symphony.

# Goosing

**Top Gun (1986)**

Be the wingman they've always wanted by straddling your
partner while imagining you're piloting a fighter jet.
A high-octane joyride that will take their breath away.

# A Taste of Cherry

**Varsity Blues (1999)**

Give your partner a tasty treat by making a whipped-cream bikini for them to lick off. Keep some extra cherries handy in case you work up an appetite.

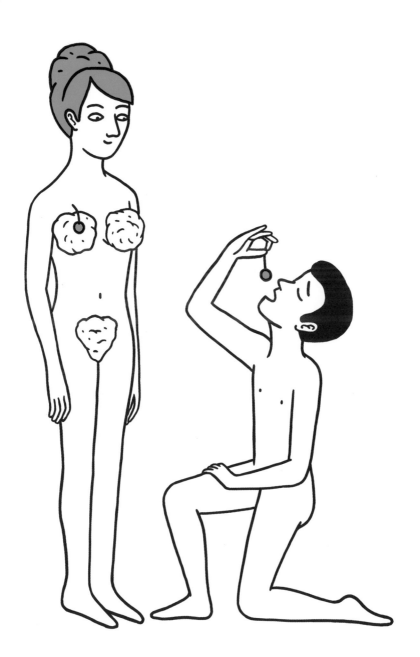

# 42

# Chest Burster

**Alien (1979)**

Use corn syrup or tomato ketchup to give your partner an authentically gory glaze. Or simply wait until it's your time of the month for a taboo-busting thrill.

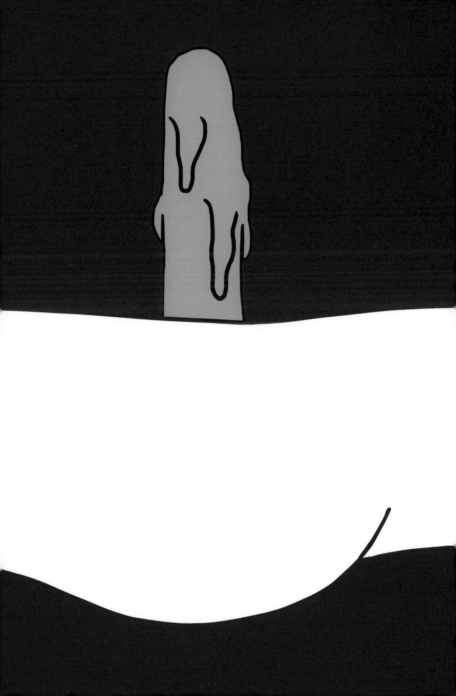

# Project Mayhem

**Fight Club (1999)**

The first rule of this ego-stroking position is to find a partner who's willing to pretend they're being penetrated by two people. There are no other rules.

# Lift Off

### An Officer and a Gentleman (1982)

As romantic gestures go, this one is a classic. Lifting your partner up, gently cradle them before lowering them onto you. Who doesn't love a happy ending?

# Rockabye

### Cry-Baby (1990)

Everyone knows that girls love a bad boy, so slick back
your hair and take your partner for a spin. Whether
you're a Square or a Drape, they won't be able to resist.

# Exquisite Corpse

**The Neon Demon (2016)**

Have your partner lay on a table or gurney and go down on them while pleasuring yourself. Turning the room temperature down will enhance the mortuary mood.

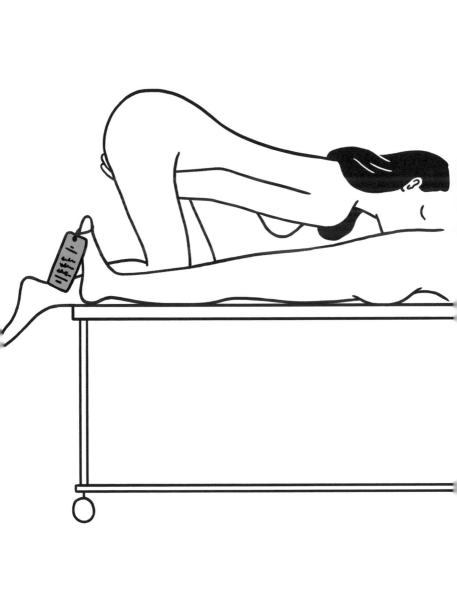

# Rain Check

**The Notebook (2004)**

Next time you get caught in a thunderstorm, hoist your partner up around your waist. You might want to move inside when things start to get really wet.

# Capote Couture

**Breakfast at Tiffany's (1961)**

They say diamonds are a girl's best friend, but pearls aren't too far behind. Just make sure they know what to expect before you present this particular necklace.

# Automatic Pilot

**Airplane! (1980)**

When all else fails, you can't go wrong with a male blow-up doll. Locate the inflation nozzle, pump it up, then when you're done simply deflate and pack away.

# Triple Word Score

**Rosemary's Baby (1968)**

Grab your favourite word-based board game and get your partner in the mood by showing off your broad vocabulary. See how many erotic words you can make.

# 51

# What a Feeling

**Flashdance (1983)**

Take your passion and make it happen by grabbing the sturdiest chair you can find and pushing yourself up on it as your partner puts their best moves on you.

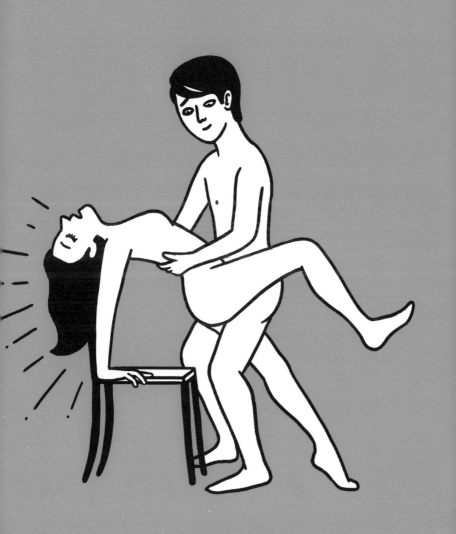

# Common Courtesy

**Full Metal Jacket (1987)**

Ensure that you're both standing to attention, then reach around and stroke your partner's soldier. Keep a steady rhythm and try to refrain from hurting their feelings.

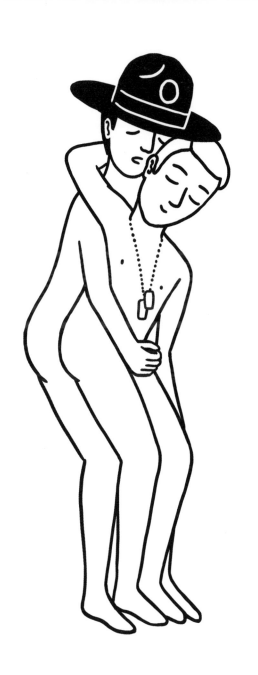

# Doctor, Doctor

**The Silence of the Lambs (1991)**

Make sure your partner is fully covered up with their arms tied, then rub yourself against them. A onesie works well if you don't happen to have a straitjacket lying around.

# Wicked Game

**Wild at Heart (1990)**

Turn the lights down low, spark up a cigarette, and let the mood take you. Slowly gyrate against each other and you'll both end up 'hotter than Georgia asphalt.'

# Hold the Phone

**Women on the Verge of a Nervous Breakdown (1988)**

Have you recenty been jilted by a lover? Tried contacting them but to no avail? Put your telephone to another use and soon you won't feel so hung up about it.

# In Too Deep

**American Psycho (2000)**

Put on your favourite 1980s pop record and set up
a camcorder to capture your threesome in close-up. You
may prefer to try this out with lovers of the easy variety.

# Kick it

## Charlie's Angels (2000)

The trick here is to avoid high-kicking your partner in the face while making sure you're close enough to quicken each other's pulses.

# Shower Time

**Psycho (1960)**

Wait until your partner is in the shower, then quietly sneak into the bathroom ready to plunge your tool into them. Guaranteed to give them a surprise they'll never forget.

# Delicious Breeze

### The Seven Year Itch (1955)

Have your partner put on their favourite cocktail dress
and turn on a desk fan for an ankle-cooling experience
that will add a touch of glamour to your sex life.

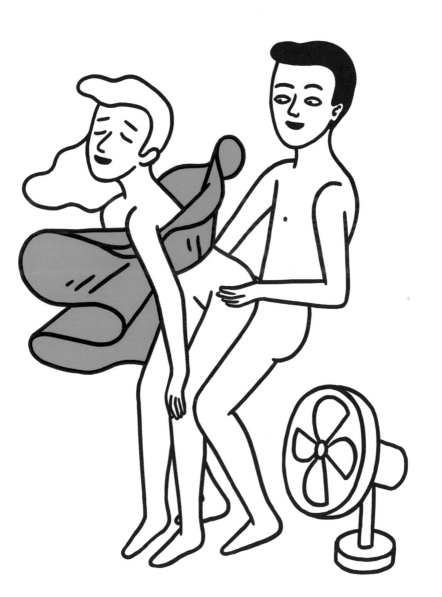

# 60

# Executive Assistant

### Secretary (2002)

Pick a safe word and park your modesty for this kinky, role-play-based position. For added enjoyment, have your partner bite down on a carrot as you spank them.

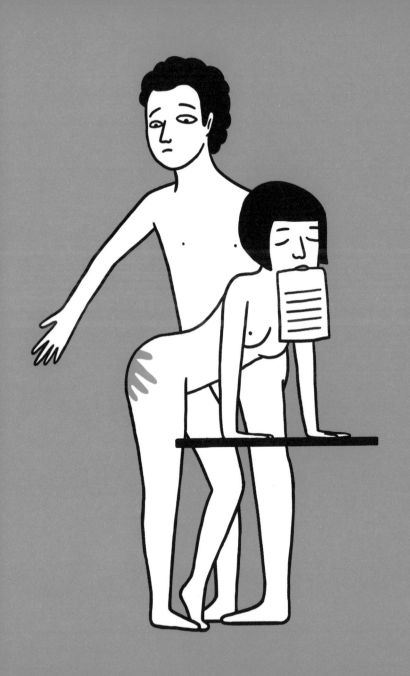

# Man in the Moon

**La Voyage Dans La Lune (1902)**

This one really isn't rocket science – you'll need to take precautionary measures to ensure that your partner enjoys themselves without compromising their eyesight.

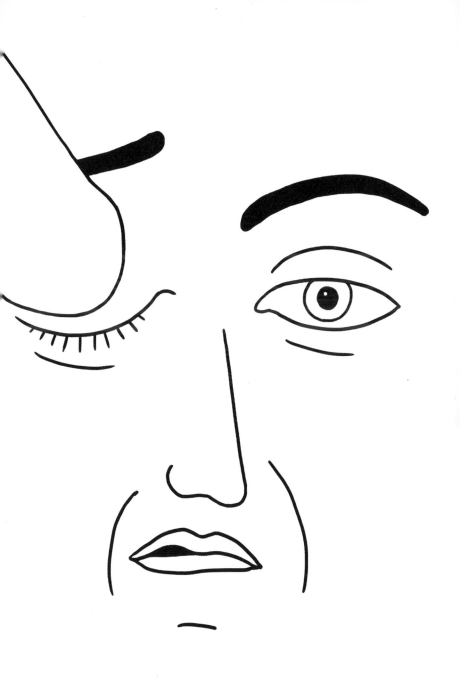

# Tunnel of Love

**Carol (2015)**

Next time you have an evening all to yourselves,
assemble an electric train set and put the engine
on course to arrive at your partner's station.

# Kiss of Death

**The Godfather: Part II (1974)**

Grab your partner around the neck and plant a
passionate kiss on them. This one is especially effective
if they've recently committed an act of betrayal.

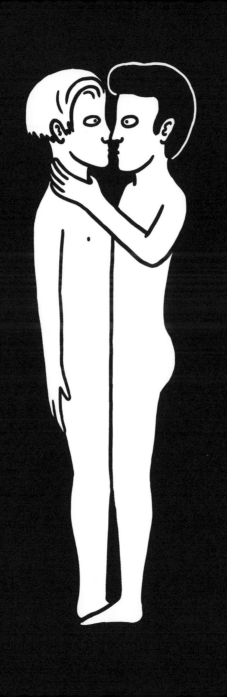

# 64

# Smooth Operator

**True Romance (1993)**

Wait until your partner is speaking on the telephone, then passionately pick them up and pin them against the wall. Just make sure they hang up before you both finish.

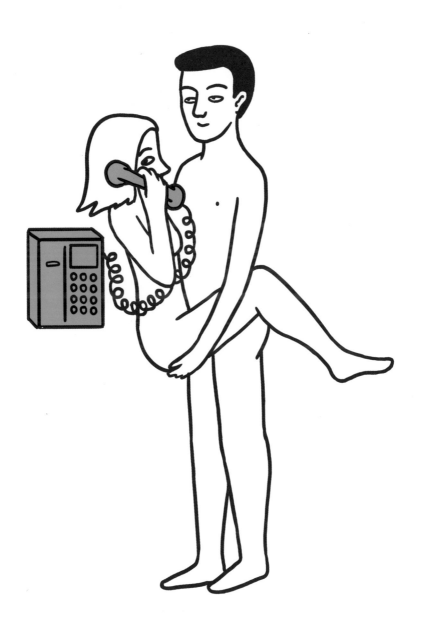

# Bullet Time

**The Matrix (1999)**

The key to this is to hold a pose as if you're moving
in super slow-motion. Then simply free your mind and
get ready to believe in the unbelievable.

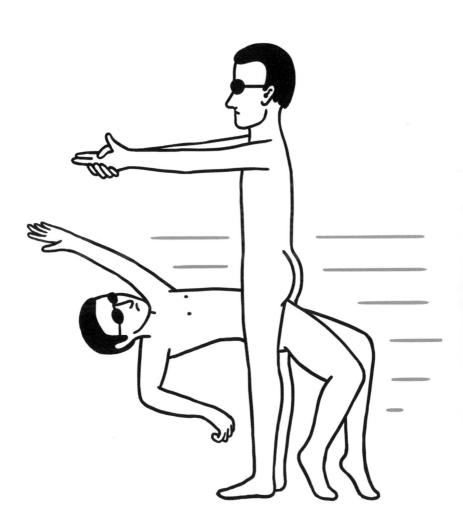

# Assassins' Tango

**Mr. & Mrs. Smith (2005)**

Marriage in a rut? Channel your inner double agent and
your life suddenly won't seem so vanilla. Check whether
your contents insurance covers acts of passion first.

# Surf's up

**Point Break (1991)**

Take up a comfortable stance, keeping your knees
bent for a real adrenaline rush. Works just as well on
dry land if you're not an experienced wave rider.

# The Ballerina

**Black Swan (2010)**

Haven't found your ideal dance partner? You won't
need one to execute this solo routine; good poise and
a smooth, sturdy handrail is all that's required.

# The Web Slinger

**Spider-Man (2002)**

While suspended upside down from a secure line,
align yourself with your partner so that you're able
to simultaneously perform oral sex on each other.

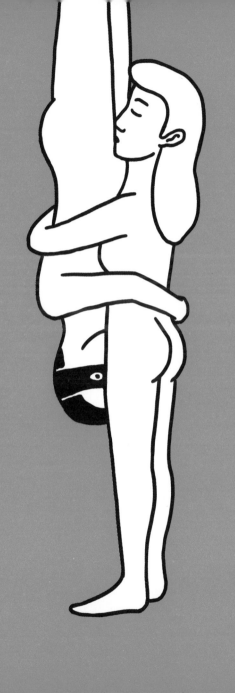

First published in 2018
by Laurence King Publishing Ltd
361–373 City Road
London EC1V 1LR
enquiries@laurenceking.com
www.laurenceking.com

This work was produced by Laurence King
Publishing Ltd, London.
Little White Lies has asserted its right under
the Copyright, Designs, and Patents Act 1988,
to be identified as the Author of this Work.

A catalogue record for this book is available
from the British Library

ISBN: 978-1-78627-214-0

Printed in Hong Kong

Design by TCOLondon
Original concept by David Jenkins and Bindi Kaufmann

*The more experimental reader might try out some
of the positions in this book. If you're horny at a
restaurant, hanging upside down and naked, or
attempting sex on a motorbike, please ensure that you
and your partner(s) have been tested for STDs and
that you practise safe sex. Always abide by the law
when doing the dirty in public and stay safe when
in compromising positions.*

FSC
www.fsc.org
MIX
Paper from
responsible sources
FSC® C001701